SHORT · SCENIC · WALKS

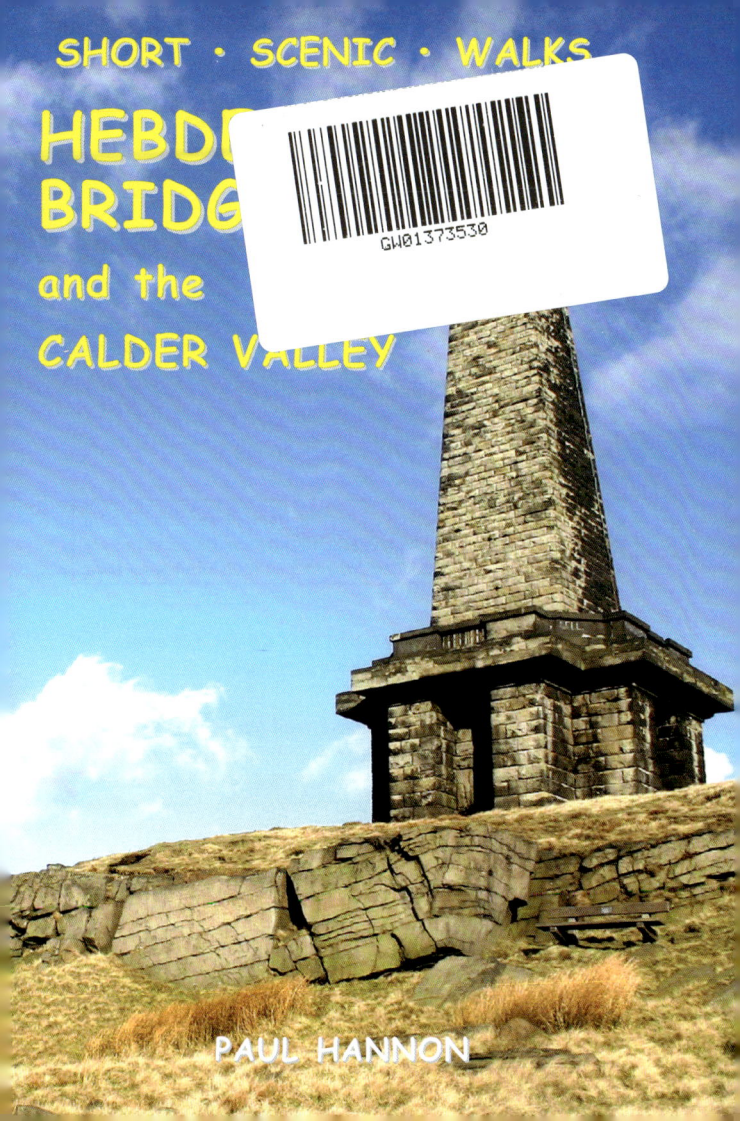

HEBDEN BRIDGE
and the
CALDER VALLEY

PAUL HANNON

HILLSIDE PUBLICATIONS
20 Wheathead Crescent
Keighley
West Yorkshire
BD22 6LX

First Published 2012

© Paul Hannon 2012

ISBN 978 1 907626 09 8

While the author has walked and researched all these routes for the purposes of this guide, no responsibility can be accepted for any unforeseen circumstances encountered whilst following them

The sketch maps are based on 1947 OS one-inch maps and earlier OS six-inch maps

Cover illustration: Packhorse trail above Lumbutts
Back cover: Staups Moor and Blackshaw Head
Page 1: Stoodley Pike
(Paul Hannon/Hillslides Picture Library)

Printed by Steffprint
Unit 5, Keighley Industrial Park
Royd Ings Avenue
Keighley
West Yorkshire
BD21 4DZ

CONTENTS

Introduction 4

1	Reddyshore Scout	8
2	Gorpley Clough	10
3	Salter Rake	12
4	Robinwood	14
5	Bride Stones	16
6	Langfield Common	18
7	Stoodley Pike	20
8	Black Hameldon	22
9	Jumble Hole Clough	24
10	Gorple Moors	26
11	Blake Dean	28
12	Graining Water	30
13	Around Colden	32
14	Crimsworth Dean	34
15	Hardcastle Crags	36
16	Heptonstall	38
17	Broadhead Clough	40
18	Withens Clough	42
19	Midgley Moor	44
20	Luddenden Dean	46

INTRODUCTION

Set in the upper valley of Yorkshire's River Calder, the characterful little town of Hebden Bridge is the focal point of the entire South Pennines. Bustling with locals and visitors, its houses climb alarmingly up steep hillsides, while in and near the lively centre are canal trips, a packhorse bridge, highly individual shops and an invaluable information centre. Although its neighbour Todmorden may offer less obvious charm, it nevertheless has much of interest, pride of place going to the splendid Town Hall of 1875.

The attraction of the upper Calder Valley is its unique blend of town and country: the two are inextricably linked, and one can revel in a feast of fascinating walking. The larger settlements squeeze into the cramped valley floor, shared with river, canal, road and railway, while steep flanks rise to intervening ledges where older villages almost shake hands across deep divides. Higher still, rough pasture gives way to wilder, open moorland.

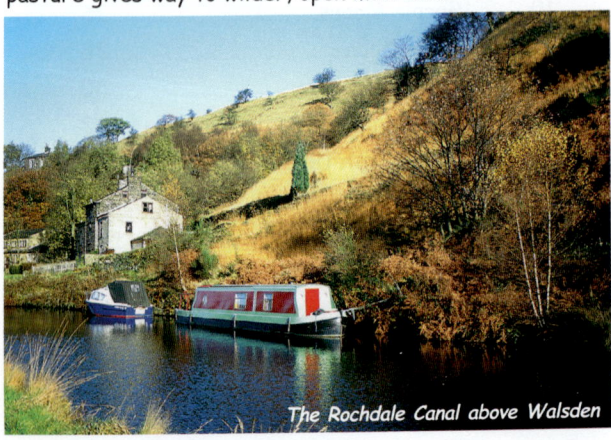

The Rochdale Canal above Walsden

The hills are laced with old packhorse routes, and many sections of stone causeway survive to be enjoyed today. Hugging the valley bottom is the Rochdale Canal, whose towpath provides miles of leisurely walking. The Calder itself, in contrast, is seen only infrequently, though it absorbs deep side valleys carved out by Luddenden Brook, Cragg Brook, Hebden Water and Walsden Water. Also tumbling to the dale floor at regular intervals are short-lived but deep-cut and richly wooded little valleys known as cloughs, where some of the earliest mills were built. Up on the tops one is never far from a reservoir, and as this is gritstone country, the higher ground is shared with clusters of boulders and crags.

Most walks are on rights of way and permissive paths with no access restrictions. Several enjoy 'Right to Roam' on areas of Open Access that can occasionally be closed, notably in the grouse shooting season: information is available from the Countryside Agency and information centres. Many walks can be accessed by public transport, so even if you come to the district by car, consider the local bus in order not to exacerbate congestion. Whilst the route description should be sufficient to guide you around each walk, a map is recommended for greater information: Ordnance Survey 1:25,000 scale maps give the finest detail, and Explorer OL21 covers all of the walks.

- Hebden Bridge Visitor & Canal Centre (01422-843831)
- Todmorden Information Centre (01706-818181)
- Open Access (0845-100 3298)
- Traveline - public transport information (0870-6082608)

HEBDEN BRIDGE and the Calder Valley

20 Short Scenic Walks

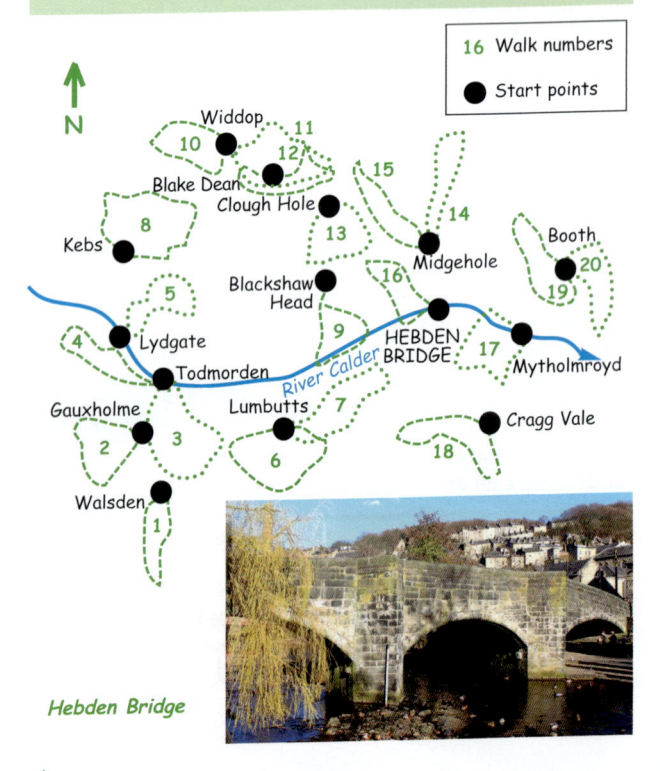

16 Walk numbers
● Start points

N ↑

- 10 Widdop
- 11
- 12
- Blake Dean
- Clough Hole
- 15
- 8 Kebs
- 13
- 14 Midgehole
- Booth
- 20
- 19
- 5
- Blackshaw Head
- 4 Lydgate
- 9
- 16
- HEBDEN BRIDGE
- 17 Mytholmroyd
- Todmorden
- River Calder
- Gauxholme
- Lumbutts
- 7
- Cragg Vale
- 2
- 3
- 6
- 18
- Walsden
- 1

Hebden Bridge

A RECORD OF YOUR WALKS

WALK	DATE	NOTES
1		
2		
3		
4		
5		
6		
7		
8		
9		
10		
11		
12		
13		
14		
15		
16		
17		
18		
19		
20		

1   REDDYSHORE SCOUT

4½ miles from Walsden

Superb walking through the impressive Walsden Gorge

Start Village centre (GR: 934219), parking near church
Map OS Explorer OL21, South Pennines

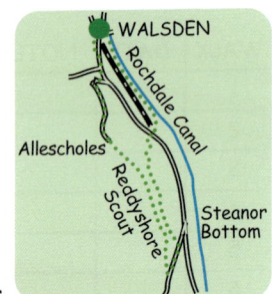

Walsden is Todmorden's southerly offshoot in the narrow valley of Walsden Water. Part of Lancashire until the late 19th century, its industrial past focused more on cotton. From the Post office head away from Todmorden on the roadside footway: parallel Square Road gives a break from the main road. Back on the main road, it bridges the railway and passes an extensive garden centre. Leave the road by turning up an enclosed path on the near side of the Waggon & Horses. At the top the surfaced Allescholes farm road is met: a broader green way opposite cuts a corner of it then follows its easier gradients. Passing the Allescholes farms, it levels out to run to a sudden demise beneath Moor Hey Farm. Alongside a small wood the old road runs to a gate onto reedy rough pasture.

A superb level track heads away, quickly passing the Allescholes milestone. Perched just off the path, it is easily missed as you stride on. This fine specimen bears distances to Todmorden, Rochdale, Burnley and Halifax. Your outward route follows this centuries-old packhorse way of Reddyshore Scout Gate high above the Summit railway tunnel. Views over the Walsden Gorge are now excellent, featuring the Rochdale Canal backed by Blackstone Edge. The mercurial green track suddenly finds itself above a craggy drop, with an air shaft by your return route below. A gate between pylons sees the way become enclosed, in part running even more dramatically atop the crest of Reddyshore Scout. Steep crags add a dramatic foreground to the views. The track shortly merges into a farm drive to drop between air shafts onto a road.

Turn left down the road as far as an air shaft. Owler Clough marks the county boundary, with an old boundary stone by the wall on the right. Briefly glimpsed on the junction below is Steanor Bottom Toll House: this hexagonal building stands astride a turnpike junction. At the boundary, meanwhile, take a gently rising green path on the left to head back towards Reddyshore Scout. This one however is to run beneath the cliffs, parallel with your outward leg. Rising to a gate/stile under a steep crag, it eases out to run beneath further crags. After a stile below a pylon it crosses to an air shaft to begin a steady descent through bracken to another shaft, just past which it meets a clearer path descending from the milestone. This drops pleasantly down the last section and on past a final shaft to join a drive: cross straight over and down a cobbled snicket to another drive joining the main road by a terrace.

Cross and go briefly left to steps down to Bottomley Road. Just to the left is the entrance to Summit Tunnel, scene of a dramatic train fire in 1984. Advance past Hilldyke Cottages to meet the Rochdale Canal at Bottomley Lock. Completed in 1804, it runs 33 miles between Manchester and Sowerby Bridge. Go left on the towpath, a splendid stride passing several locks descending into Walsden. The Cross Keys comes just a minute from the end, where at Travis Mill Lock you join a road alongside tall-spired St Peter's church, turning left on St Peter's Gate to finish.

Warland and the canal from Reddyshore Scout

2   GORPLEY CLOUGH

**3¼ miles
from Gauxholme**

**Quiet moorland paths and
a splendid wooded clough**

Start Viaduct (GR: 929231),
junction of A681 a short mile
south of Todmorden centre: parking on Bacup Road
Map OS Explorer OL21, South Pennines

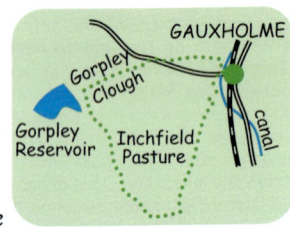

At Gauxholme a long, low railway viaduct straddles the main junction, with the Masons Arms and a craft brewery beneath. From the main road pass under the viaduct, past the pub and over the canal bridge. Quickly turn left on short-lived Naze Road, and from a gate on the left alongside modern housing, a broad green track heads away. Doubling back almost immediately, a steep climb of The Naze ensues, featuring a cleverly engineered, enjoyable zigzag. This ensuing mile traces an old packhorse route from Todmorden towards Rochdale. The map-like view of the cramped valley floor with its railway, road, canal and mills, is in very stark contrast with the hillside's crumbling walls and reedy pastures.

As the gradient eases the climb continues between old walls to a brief enclosed section onto open moor. Go forward to join a wide track, and briefly left on it. As it bears left at a wall corner take the lesser fork straight ahead, a stone causeway gently rising arrow-like across the moorland of Inchfield Pasture. At a stream crossing the path deteriorates a little, but forges on to join the broad, unsurfaced Foul Clough Road by Thorns Greece Farm. Turn right, rising gently to a brow then curving right into a minor clough. Here a slender path is signed right, rising very gently alongside the reedy beginnings. Marker posts ensure the little path can't be lost, and only moderately moist patches are encountered as you gain a brow, with a line of tall pylons by the steeper slopes of Oatley Hill to the left. Massive views look over Upper Calderdale's moorland, and Gorpley Reservoir appears in its fold of the hills as the path drops gently away. More steeply it drops to the base of the final pylon in front of wooded Gorpley Clough. A green track runs the final paces to a gate in a wall, bridging an outflow from the reservoir then dropping right on an enclosed course along the base of the grassy dam to approach the treatment plant.

Alongside it take a small gate on the right to descend a part-stepped path (not the steep steps right) into Gorpley Clough, a charming wooded dell whose tinkling stream enjoys some enchanting moments. This same path leads unerringly down, crossing and re-crossing the stream to finally emerge onto the Bacup road at a parking area. Turn briefly right on the footway past an old mill, then escape at a gap on the left beyond a house. A path rises through Stones Wood, leaving by a kissing-gate after a small clough. The path crosses two fields to a junction of old green ways: rise left between walls, and through the gate/stile at the top turn right to cross a field bottom. From a stile at the end go on past a stable block at Watty Farm, and just past the house is a wall-stile accessing a minuscule green way. A few strides to the left this meets a steep path that is dramatically perched above the valley, with an amazing bird's-eye view. Turn down the broadening path to finish, emerging onto Pexwood Road just short of the main road.

In Gorpley Clough

SALTER RAKE

4¼ miles from Todmorden

From towpath to moor top, easy to follow paths include a historic packhorse route

Start Town centre
(GR: 936241), car parks
Map OS Explorer OL21,
South Pennines

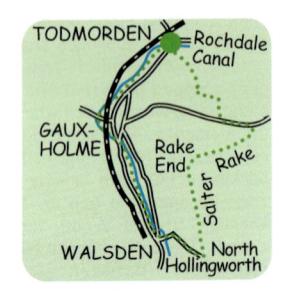

From the central roundabout outside the Town Hall, head south on the Rochdale road the short way to the Golden Lion at Fielden Square, bridging the Rochdale Canal en route. Cross the side road to Honey Hole Road: rising steeply away, it jinks beneath the tall-spired Unitarian Church, climbs past the clustered houses of Honey Hole and then a sharp kink takes it above the churchyard. With a grassy centre it pulls steeply up to some cottages. The unsurfaced continuation bears left, more gently now between walls. Ahead is the moorland skyline of Langfield Common, with the sturdy monument on Stoodley Pike further left. The lane swings sharp left to a junction by Longfield equestrian centre where keep right to rise onto the Lumbutts-Gauxholme moorland road.

Go left on a short, very gentle rise to the Shepherd's Rest pub. Immediately opposite, take a gate onto the open moorland of Langfield Common. A grassy track heads away, but within a minute meets the well-preserved causeway of Salter Rake, part of a packhorse route used for bringing salt across the Pennines from Cheshire. Turn right on this, rising gently to a gateway off the moor. The walled way rises away, noting an old inscribed guidestone on the left partway up. You soon re-emerge onto open moorland above the house at Shurcrack. With massive open views over the rough moors surrounding Todmorden, the causey immediately resumes its superb, gently angled course up across the unkempt moor, curving left at the end up onto a brow. The summit of the walk at around 985ft/300m is marked by a path crossroads at Rake End.

Your way is straight on, starting a steady slant down the moor, the stone flags soon returning as you look down on Walsden's steep valley. This grand stride ultimately enters walled confines at North Hollingworth. Joining a drive at this little hamlet, advance briefly to a junction. With a splendid white-walled house in front, go right on Hollingworth Lane descending steeply to the valley. At the bottom it passes above an abandoned section of road and doubles back down to the edge of Walsden. A house on the right dated 1805 was the residence of Nobel prize-winning scientist Sir John Cockcroft (1897-1967). Passing the tall-spired St Peter's church it runs on to meet the Rochdale Canal again. Across it turn right on the towpath, which is traced all the way back into Todmorden.

Interest along the way includes quite a number of locks, and also Walsden Water running parallel for a lengthy spell: a chippy is handily placed. The only break of note comes when the main road intervenes: rise to cross both it and the canal before resuming on the opposite bank. An aqueduct carries the canal over the beck, then approaching the Bacup road you pass under a rail bridge at the Gauxholme arches: the Masons Arms stands by the viaduct just a few strides off the route. Continuing under the Bacup road the railway soon crosses back above, and nearer the end an enormous brick wall opposite supports the railway. Here you curve round to rejoin the road on which you began alongside intriguing Library Lock, whose vertical bottom gate permits boats' access beneath the main road.

The Rochdale Canal at Gauxholme

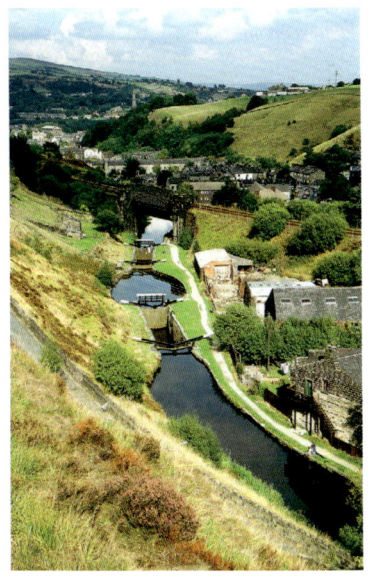

13

4   ROBINWOOD

*4½ miles
from Todmorden*

**Woodland and moorland valley
flanks of the upper dale**

Start Town centre
(GR: 936241), car parks
Map OS Explorer OL21, South Pennines

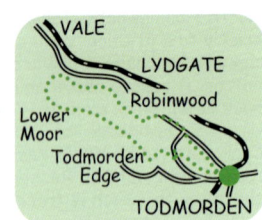

    From the roundabout head south on the Rochdale road, quickly turning up Rise Lane on the right. On the left is Todmorden Hall, built in 1603. Continue up past the station and under the rail bridge. The road climbs steeply away, but almost at once take the steep Ridge Steps up onto Well Lane. Virtually opposite, a broad, surfaced path heads off into trees. Ignoring lesser branches, this runs all the way to a fork above an open area of park: the unsurfaced left branch slants gently up to a narrow road, Ewood Lane.

    Turn briefly left then take a path doubling back right for a long, steady pull through a beechwood. At the top is a grand level section before being deposited into a field: super views are enjoyed over the valley. Go left up the wallside, becoming enclosed to rise to a rough access road at Todmorden Edge. Go briefly right, and take the first of adjacent gates on the left opposite the last building. Rise away along the wallside, a part-enclosed section being sunken and moist. Emerging, don't go to the far end, but take a gate on the right to resume on the wall's other side, with a fence taking over at a stile. From a gate at the end bear left up the field to a gate opposite, passing through sheep pens onto Lower Moor.

    Advance the few strides up onto a drive, and bear right past a reedy pool. Ignore an immediate branch down to a house, and keep on to the next house. Directly above it, leave the track for a thin path slanting onto the moor. It quickly levels out to meet a cross-paths: keep right to contour along not far above the track, passing above another renovated farmhouse and on to approach the final one. During this a broader path slants up from the right to merge, and rises slightly to run on until above the last house. Here your path fragments at a crossroads with a sunken way coming in from the left. Slant down to the wall just past the house, and advance to a corner just beyond. Turn down a reedy, walled way, emerging to drop to the ruin of Roundfield. Continue down the wallside to a stile off the moor bottom. Remain with the right-hand crumbling wall to drop quickly onto the crest of a path dropping both left and right, divided by a near vertical tiny sidestream between heathery flanks. Keep right to curve round to a promontory above the valley: with Pudsey Clough opposite, this is a fine moment.

This super path slants beneath craggy Barewise Wood to the valley. Emerging onto a drive at a bridge, don't cross to the road but take an access road right. At the house gates, don't enter the drive but take a gate/stile on the right, and a rough path rises beneath scattered Robin Wood. This improves above a pond and runs on beneath a wall, rising slightly to a stile at the end. Two faint paths head away: take the left one rising slightly, then running on through a part-wooded hollow before rising to a broader green path. Turn down this to a stile into woods, and a fine path slants down to the rear of Scaitcliff Hall, then left down to the main road at Gate Bottom. Go right past a school and Ewood Lane to enter Centre Vale Park, emerging at the far end to continue the final minutes into the centre.

The path beneath Barewise Wood

15

5   BRIDE STONES

4 miles from Lydgate

Superb rock formations and historic hillside packways

Start *Post office (GR: 923255), 1½ miles north of Todmorden centre on A646 Burnley road: street parking*

Map *OS Explorer OL21, South Pennines*

      Leave the main road by Church Road at the Post office/shop, and at the end bear right on Owlers Walk. A path passes right of the last house and on beneath a rail embankment to an immense arch. Pass underneath it on a drive, then a small gate on the right sends steps climbing to a gate. Resume up a fieldside, and when the fence goes left go straight up a distinct hollow to Rake Farm. Go right of the house onto the drive, then pass behind the house to a gate. An old way rises above the garden to an intriguing corner stile: Whirlaw rises impressively back over the house. Don't use the stile but remain on the path slanting right to a small gate into a walled way. This climbs then runs left to another bend in front of the open country of Stannally Stones.

      Climb again to emerge onto a drive at a house. Passing left of it another walled way curves up to the old packhorse track of Stony Lane, with big Calderdale views. Turn right for a grand stride, emerging onto a reedy pasture to a gate onto Whirlaw Common. Take the right-hand of two flagged paths heading away: curving beneath Whirlaw Stones it remains flagged until becoming enclosed. A little further, above East Whirlaw Farm, double back left up a wallside track. This swings right above the wall and climbs further, closing in on the wall again to rise to a gate with a carved gatepost at the top right corner. Ascend initially steep Windy Harbour Lane past Windy Harbour Farm, levelling out at a mast to run on to Eastwood Road. Go left as far as the end of the left-hand wall, where a stile sends a path across Bride Stones Moor to the outcrops of the same name. The Great Bride Stones are an extensive group of rocks, and the first ones include a remarkable detached rock. An OS column at 1437ft/438m looks over. Advance on either the base or crest of the main rocks, where rock climbers may be in action.

Beyond the end of the immediate main cluster, a faint way angles down and along to a big rock, then drop left to an overhanging rock just above a fence-stile. Don't cross, but take a path right, dropping down above the fence towards Bride Stones Farm. Before it the path drops left between fence and wall to a stile in a wall at the bottom. A thin trod winds down colourful slopes close by an old wall, veering slightly away from it to a stile back onto Stony Lane. Turn right on a brief rise, then over a stream and up more broadly to a brow. Leave here by a gate/stile on the left, on a wall-side track down towards Orchan Rocks. Part way down you can opt for a stile on the right, a few strides beyond which a thin path drops to meet a sunken level path curving round to the top of the rocks, a grand location. Drop down either side and go left to rejoin the track at a stile. At the bottom corner is a gateway: through it drop left to meet another track in a corner. Through a gate it become enclosed, absorbing a drive down through Kitson Wood. As civilisation is embraced turn left after the first house on a cart track to a steep access road down onto the street where you began.

The Bride Stones

6 — LANGFIELD COMMON

*3¾ miles
from Lumbutts*

A fine high-level march around the Lumbutts and Mankinholes skyline, only modest effort needed

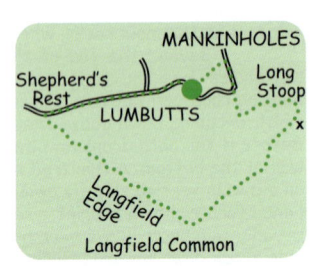

Start Hamlet centre (GR: 956234), roadside parking between Top Brink pub and Methodist church
Map OS Explorer OL21, South Pennines

Lumbutts nestles in a hollow dominated by an old water wheel tower that served a cotton mill. Immediately above is Lee Dam, one of three tree-lined dams hovering above the hamlet, scene of an annual New Year 'dip'. From the pub descend either the enclosed setted path or the road by the tower and head west along the endlessly rising road beneath the moor. En route note a sundial dated 1864 on a cottage. After a long threequarter-mile the Shepherd's Rest pub is reached. From a gate on the left follow a good track doubling steadily back up the moor. Almost at once a splendidly flagged packhorse route is crossed. Before long a steeper right branch to rocks above is ignored: keep to the gentler left one to rise to old workings. Now narrower but totally foolproof, the path rises ever gradually beneath the dark cliffs of Langfield Edge, with its shapely rock formations and scars of long abandoned quarrying. Your path is carried across the successive embankments of two old dams beneath the quarries.

Eventually this superbly engineered way gains the far end of the rocks, then a path contours around the head of Black Clough and doubles back across the far side. Throughout this entire moorland section sweeping views look across upper Calderdale, full of colour and interest in contrast to the flat moors to your right. The path remains clear as it begins a gentle rise above a well-defined edge enhanced by a rash of boulders. As the slope eases so do the rocks, and the path skirts the top of Coldwell Hill to drop gently past a prominent cairn to merge with the Pennine Way. Bear left on its part-flagged course past a seat on a slight drop before rising slightly to a crossroads with a well-preserved paved way.

This is overseen by the mighty Long Stoop, an old guidepost where the Pennine Way meets a centuries-old packhorse route. The splendidly preserved section of flags can be seen going all the way down towards Mankinholes, so turn left to do just that. Quickly doubling back left the old way slants infallibly down the moor to a wall corner, then shadows the wall down to the moor bottom. From the right-hand gate head away on a level, walled track into the little hamlet of Mankinholes. This old handloom weaving settlement has great water troughs as a sign of its importance in packhorse days. Most visitors today are youth hostellers breaking their Pennine Way journey in the shadow of Stoodley Pike. Keep straight on to the last buildings, and on as far as a lone house at the site of Mankinholes Methodist Church. Here turn left down splendidly paved Lumbutts Lane to return unfailingly to Lumbutts. At the foot of the lane is an old guidepost inscribed 'Halifax' and 'Heptonstall'.

The Long Stoop

7 — STOODLEY PIKE

4½ miles from Lumbutts

A high-level stroll to an iconic landmark

Start *Hamlet centre (GR: 956234), roadside parking between Top Brink pub and Methodist church*
Map *OS Explorer OL21, South Pennines*

Lumbutts nestles in a hollow dominated by an old water wheel tower that served a cotton mill. Immediately above is Lee Dam, one of three tree-lined dams hovering above the hamlet, scene of an annual New Year 'dip'. From the pub follow the road rising past the tower, out of the hamlet to a bend by the Methodist church. Here take a walled track on the right, rapidly swinging uphill on an unerring climb (latterly flagged) to a gate onto the foot of the open moor. Here a magnificent flagged former packhorse trod rises away with a wall, and when the wall parts company the way slants ever upwards, enjoying fine views to the monument and out across the valley. Near the top it doubles back right to arrive at a path crossroads with the Pennine Way, overseen by the Long Stoop, an old guidepost of monumental stature.

Abandon the flags and turn left on the path rising gently past the stoop and through an old quarry to then follow a broad and popular course through clusters of rocks to Stoodley Pike. The monument was erected in 1815 to celebrate peace after victory over Napoleon, but later collapsed and was replaced by a new tower in 1856. An inscription over the door explains some of its history. It stands a mighty 120ft/36m above the 1312ft/400m moor top, and is the upper valley's most famous landmark. A dark, spiral staircase climbs 39 steps to a viewing balcony: the 360 degree panorama features moorland skylines in almost every direction, with intervening slopes masking the industrialised valley floor.

Leave the top with the Pennine Way striking eastwards, the broad path passing a spring bursting into a stone trough. At a wall-gap the reinforced path runs a few strides further with a wall to a gateway in it, then drops down below the Doe Stones. Dropping onto a broad, level track at a crossroads with the Pennine Bridleway go left on it, and after passing through a gate it runs a largely level course beneath the Pike's steep slopes. This old track is known as London Road, and leads unfailingly along the foot of the common to eventually reach a corner. Keep straight on the walled track in front to drop down to the edge of Mankinholes. This old handloom weaving settlement largely by-passed by the 20th century has great water troughs as a sign of its importance in packhorse days. Most visitors today are youth hostellers breaking their Pennine Way journey in the shadow of the pike.

Turn right through the hamlet to the last buildings, and on as far as a lone house at the site of Mankinholes Methodist Church. Here turn left down the splendidly paved Lumbutts Lane to return unfailingly to the start at Lumbutts. At the foot of the lane note an old stone guidepost inscribed 'Halifax' and 'Heptonstall', complete with mileages.

Approaching Stoodley Pike

8 — BLACK HAMELDON

4¾ miles from Kebs

A wild walk to the Pennine watershed

Start Junction of Mount Lane and Kebs Road (GR: 914275), 3 miles west of Blackshaw Head on Long Causeway
Map OS Explorer OL21, South Pennines
Access Open Access land, see page 5

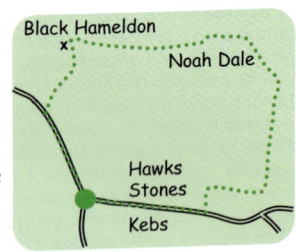

Head east along the road towards Hawks Stones for a lengthy stroll, passing beneath the eponymous bouldery edge on the skyline. Beyond scattered dwellings you approach the Sportsmans Arms. From a stile on the left just before its car park a good path heads off across moorland. It crosses to a fork just short of an embankment, on which turn right, the length of the former Redmires Dam. At the far end advance moistly to a fence ahead in front of a feeble plantation, and turn right to a corner stile. Resume as before along the edge of sparse trees, passing a pond to emerge by curious buildings: to your right is an air traffic navigation beacon at Pole Hill. Keep on the drive to a T-junction with a firm track, Dukes Cut. Go left along to a fork, with a house hidden to the right. Ignore this and keep on with an old wall to a minor brow, with Black Hameldon on the left skyline and Noah Dale below.

The track becomes enclosed by old walls and swings right to drop gently to a track crossroads at Four Gates End. Ignoring all options, a stile on the left sends a bright little path down the moorside with an old wall to the right. Degenerating slightly it leads down to an arched bridge on Noah Dale Water, and across a small embankment is a short rise to another junction of ways. Turn left for a part sunken slant above the ruins of Pad Laithe and Noah Dale. Above the second ruins the way ends at a stile onto rough moorland. From here the path is waymarked all the way to the top.

Continue along the old wall/fence side as far as the wall corner, where the path bears left to the end of the former Noah Dale dam wall. Probably built to serve mills down the valley, there were also lead mines nearby. The thin path runs on the near side of the old reservoir, and after bridging a small stream starts to ascend the slope ahead. A few faint strides point left to a stile in a fence climbing the hill, and across it a grassy ditch makes a perfect ascent route. When the ditch falters ignore a stile back over the fence and remain on your thin path, over easing ground and past scattered rocks to the watershed on Black Hameldon. An OS column stands at 1571ft/479m on the summit, Hoof Stones Height. Surrounded by scattered rocks, Coal Clough windfarm is startlingly close just below. Otherwise, the surrounds are almost exclusively moorland.

Leave by heading sharp left, southwards. Across some peat a thin path forms, and odd marker posts guide it the few minutes to the top of a distinct boundary ditch. This quickly leads down to a cluster of rocks, the Wolf Stones. From here the ditch broadens considerably and drops more markedly as a grassy way between rougher moorland. When reeds start to fill it, keep to the right edge and an intermittent little path can be traced surprisingly quickly down to the road, dropping to gain it by a kissing-gate at a lay-by by the bridge on the county boundary. Go left to finish.

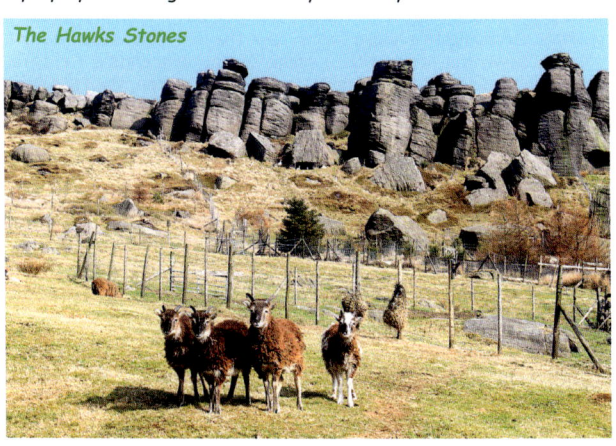

The Hawks Stones

9 — JUMBLE HOLE CLOUGH

*4¾ miles
from Blackshaw Head*

**Exploring a fascinating
side valley: hilly stuff!**

Start *Hamlet centre
(GR: 958275), roadside parking*
Map *OS Explorer OL21,
South Pennines*

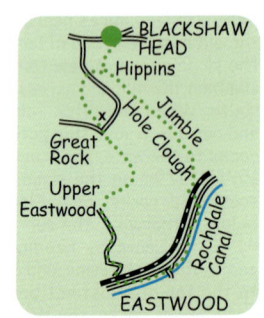

At 1115ft/340m the walk's start is its high point, with big views over the valley to Stoodley Pike. From an old milestone at the central junction head on Badger Lane only as far as the end of the Methodist church graveyard. Here go right down a short drive, forking right in front of a house to a lower house. Entering the yard behind, bear right on a flagged wallside path down into a reedy pasture. Dropping to a house below, take the left-hand stile into the garden. Down the house side a stone causey descends a fieldside onto a drive. Cross over and down outside the garden, then straight down between fields to a stile at another house. Drop down its left side, and a short, enclosed green way drops to a path junction just short of the lovely house at Hippins, with a 1656 datestone.

Immediately before the house take a kissing-gate on the left to follow a wallside path away. An early stile in it is the point to branch right, a path forming to descend steps to a footbridge in Jumble Hole Clough: note the waterslide immediately downstream. Turn down to ruined Staups Mill: lower down you will see further remains of mill workings. Leaving the mill the path rises briefly, but part way up take a left fork to remain parallel with but high above the beck. Passing above a substantial crag the path descends to cross an angled cross-paths and then along the edge of two fields, returning to denser woods to merge into a descending drive. Below a millpond it doubles back to cross the beck, then clings to its bank to run by mill ruins to Jumble Hole, overlooked by a tall chimney.

Before the first houses cross a footbridge on the right into a field, tracing the right-hand wall to a brow with a welcome seat. Continue on to a corner in front of Mulcture Hall, squeezing into the garden top to join an access road. Turn down to the next hairpin and go right on a path between trees and railway. A footbridge crosses the line and down onto the main road at Eastwood. Go briefly right then cross to escape on Burnt Acres Lane, crossing the Calder to the Rochdale Canal at another bridge: turn right for a splendid towpath stroll. A road briefly interrupts at Holmcoat Bridge and Lock, where the path resumes. A milestone precedes Stoodley Bridge, under which turn right onto an access road which is followed left, over the Calder to Victoria Terrace, rising left onto the main road.

Cross to the footway and go left to soon escape right up East Lee Lane under a rail arch. Rising steeply above a wooded clough, it eases out to slant up between fields to Lower East Lee, then up to fork into access roads at another house, Mount Pleasant. Bear right behind it, but leave within a few strides by an enclosed path left of the drive. Rising to houses (Chapel House), turn right onto a grassy area behind them, crossing to a stile into a field. Head away, slanting slightly left in the third field to a corner stile, resuming along a wall top onto an access road. Turn up this for a fair pull that culminates on joining a road beneath the mighty Great Rock on its heathery common: scramble to the top and enjoy the view. A green lane to its left puts you onto heathery Staups Moor. A path continues with the right-hand wall, crossing a track and stile at the end into a reedy pasture to drop onto a road. Cross Hippins Bridge to turn right on a drive to Hippins, from where retrace steps back to the start.

Great Rock

10   GORPLE MOORS

4 miles from Widdop

Good paths and tracks around a trio of windswept moorland reservoirs

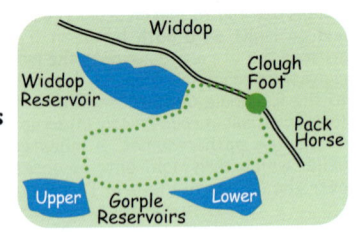

Start Clough Foot (GR: 946323), roadside parking area half-mile west of Pack Horse Inn
Map OS Explorer OL21, South Pennines
Access Open Access land, see page 5

From the lay-by take the gate across the road and head away along the inviting reservoir road which curves up and around to the dam of Gorple Lower Reservoir. Don't cross, but take the right branch to continue alongside the water and its feeder Reaps Water. Remain on this until rising to the dam of the second sheet of water, Gorple Upper Reservoir. En route you encounter several stands of trees, some patches of heather, and a wooden shooters' cabin with the impressive array of Dicken Rocks ranged up the moorland slope behind. The two Gorple Reservoirs were completed in 1934.

Again don't cross the dam, instead cross the small drain just before it on the right and take a thin path climbing directly up the slope of Shuttleworth Moor. Initially steep, it soon eases to rise through various outcrops, some of these rock formations being impressively substantial. The Gorple Stones are high on the skyline ahead left. The path continues up this broad tongue to join a wide track, Gorple Gate. At around 1410ft/430m the walk's high point is astride an old way over the moors to Worsthorne in Lancashire, and would have been at its busiest in packhorse days. Big views look west to the moors south of Burnley, while eastwards the Pack Horse Inn looks diminutive amid a Calderdale landscape looking towards Stoodley Pike.

Turn right along the track, which at once begins a gentle descent. Widdop Reservoir soon appears in its entirety ahead, backed by a high craggy edge. After dropping steeply left to a hairpin bend, ignore a thinner path bearing left and remain on your main track. This slants down towards the reservoir, passing beneath a small plantation to near the shore. This leads along to the end, crossing the embankment out onto the road. Widdop Reservoir was built to supply Halifax and was completed in 1878, over 50 years before the walk's two other reservoirs: it almost equals their joint capacity. Materials reached the site by means of a 5½-mile long horse-drawn tramway from further down the valley. Outstanding crags flank the reservoir to the north.

Go right on this largely unfenced moor road, past Clough Foot to the start. The moorland Heptonstall-Colne road was an important trans-Pennine packhorse route some three centuries ago, lime and cloth being major goods carried. Shortly after leaving the dam, look back over your right shoulder to see a giant 'rocking' stone perched on one of the moor edge buttresses at Cludders Slack.

Widdop Reservoir   *Dicken Rocks*

11 — BLAKE DEAN

3½ miles from Widdop

Good paths above lovely streams in colourful open country

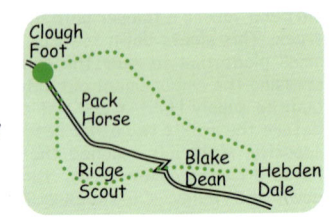

Start Clough Foot (GR: 946323), roadside parking area half-mile west of Pack Horse Inn
Map OS Explorer OL21, South Pennines

From the lay-by follow the road south-east towards the pub, appropriately named as it stands astride an important pack-horse route. However, beyond a lone house take a bridle-gate on the right into a short-lived green way. At the end go left with a crumbling wall along the edge of the deep little clough. The path soon reaches a fork. The right branch sends a flagged path down to a charming watersmeet in the narrow valley bottom of Graining Water: it is well seen from above. Your route keeps straight on by the wall. A thinner path skirts the pronounced drop, becoming clearer when the old wall parts company and the gritstone outcrops of Ridge Scout appear. Beyond the first boulders the path starts a gentle descent, slanting more into denser bracken after a second, larger group, then running on beneath the largest outcrops to a stile back onto a hairpin bend of the road.

Graining Water above Blake Dean

28

The building in front is on the site of Blake Dean Baptist Chapel (1802): the burial ground survives alongside. Turn down to the bridge and take a drive on the left before it, leaving it at the first opportunity as a stile sends a stone-stepped path down to a footbridge on Alcomden Water in Blake Dean. This is the archetypal beauty spot, another colourful watersmeet with grassy banks and green islands beneath steep bracken and gritstone-studded slopes. Take the path climbing away, and when a broad green path comes along from a former railway cutting, turn right along it. Shortly, down below, five footings can clearly be seen: these supported a 700ft/215m long trestle viaduct which carried a steam-powered railway 100ft/30m above the beck. The course of the line is also clearly discernible. It was constructed in 1901 in order to transport materials to the reservoir site in Walshaw Dean.

Approaching a stile at the end, instead bear left up a thinner path rising near the fence, soon easing out to reach a small gate in it as it meets a wall. A thin, clear path heads off through an old gateway, running a pleasant course along the top of a wooded bank. Shortly emerging from the trees into an open area with big views down-dale, at once take a small gate in the adjacent wall, and ascend two fieldsides to a gate onto a firm access road by the house at New Laithe Farm. Turn left on this for a long, level stride, emerging into the open to run on and then down to meet Alcomden Water again at Holme Ends. Across the stone-arched bridge ascend the other side, quickly reaching an open area. Fork left to join the surfaced Walshaw Dean reservoir road, which runs left back to the start: a plantation shadows you up over a brow. Dropping onto a bend just before reaching the road, a bridle-gate on the left cuts out a small corner to gain the lay-by.

Blake Dean

12   GRAINING WATER

**3½ miles
from Blake Dean**

**Super walking above two
rugged side valleys**

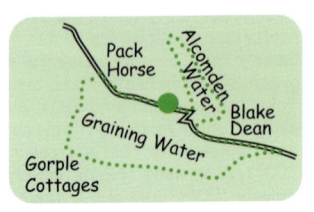

*Start Blake Dean (GR: 957314), signed parking area
at top of zigzags half a mile east of Pack Horse Inn
Map OS Explorer OL21, South Pennines
Access Open Access land, see page 5*

Begin by following the gently rising road west to the Pack Horse Inn. Not having earned a drink yet, continue half a minute further and from a ladder-stile on the left descend an old wallside to a stile onto a path overlooking Graining Water. Go 30 strides left then fork right down a superb, largely flagged old path to the clough floor. Just downstream is a charming watersmeet in a lovely spot, marked by footbridges crossing both streams in the shadow of a frowning crag. Across the second bridge the path climbs steeply away, soon easing to rise up the grassy moor, much of it stone-flagged. Gorple Lower Reservoir's grassy dam appears over to the right.

*Alcomden Water
at Holme Ends*

The footpath climbs to meet an access road just short of isolated Gorple Cottages, the old reservoir keepers' houses. Turn left on this for a superb level

30

promenade along the moor in the company of an unseen drain. The views are magnificent as you run parallel with Ridge Scout across the divide of Graining Water, overtopped by the Pack Horse beneath long moorland skylines. The way later slants steadily down to emerge onto the road at Widdop Gate. Double back left down this to enjoy splendid views over hugely colourful Blake Dean at your feet.

Immediately over the bridge at the bottom take a small gate on the right, and a few steps send a path down to Graining Water, and quickly downstream to a footbridge on the main beck, Alcomden Water. This is the archetypal beauty spot, another delectable watersmeet with grassy banks and green islands beneath steep bracken and gritstone-studded slopes. Take the path climbing away, and when a broad green path comes in from the left from a former railway cutting, double back left on its course. Here ran a steam powered railway, constructed in 1901 to transport materials to the reservoir site in Walshaw Dean.

A slight rise through knolls precedes a grand level stride above the rim of the colourful little clough of Alcomden Water. This runs on to join a firm access road, dropping left to meet Alcomden Water again at Holme Ends. Across the stone-arched bridge double back left downstream, a thin path quickly forming above the wall and crossing a steepening bank, through an old wall to a gap-stile on the right, joining an enclosed lane. Go briefly left down this then take steps on the right up to a small gate (not the stile on the right). From here the path runs a splendid, corresponding return course again above the clough, always on the bank top to reach a corner stile in front of trees at the end. This puts you onto the top of the hairpins, and thus the end.

The Pack Horse from across Graining Water

13   AROUND COLDEN

**3¾ miles
from Clough Hole**

**A wedge of moorland
divides deep wooded valleys**

Start *National Trust car park
(GR: 969297), on Widdop
road a long mile and a half
past Heptonstall*   Map *OS Explorer OL21, South Pennines*

    Joining the road, go left for two minutes to Greenwood Lee, a yeoman clothier's house of 1712. Opposite, take a stile on the right into a slender pasture, entering a field where a thin trod rises right to a gate/stile halfway up. This puts you onto Heptonstall Moor, and a thin path rises left with the wall to a cross-paths at the top. Cross and rise left to another wall, ascending the moorside to meet the Pennine Way at Mount Pleasant. The path goes on over the brow, where a cairn marks your high point at 1200ft/366m. This fine tract of heather moorland enjoys big views, especially the northerly moorland sweep from Gorple Stones to Midgley Moor.

    Keep straight on to drop towards a final corner of moorland: advance on the main path, and as it drops left to a corner gate, instead take a thin trod slanting right to a corner stile just below. Ahead are views over Colden to Stoodley Pike. Entering green pastures head away with an old wall on your left, dropping into an enclosed footway. This joins a drive, with a road just below. A few steps right take a stile opposite and descend the fieldside, largely on an old paved way. Just short of the bottom it swings left to a stile onto a road. Turn right down through Colden, past the school to Jack Bridge and the New Delight pub.

    Just up the road behind it, turn left at a hairpin bend along a driveway. Ignoring a right branch keep on above a house, becoming a pleasant bridleway above Colden Clough. A tract of open country develops, and soon a thinner path drops down the heathery bank to Hebble Hole Bridge. This ancient stone-slabbed footbridge occupies a charming location on a former panniermans' way. Across it the path slants right, up to a fork. Take the better-flagged path running right, between fields and the drop to the beck. Entering Foster Wood a stile is met at a kink in the accompanying wall, and here the causey vacates the beck's environs to cross several fields. Heptonstall church appears ahead, along with more of Colden Clough. When the flags end the path becomes enclosed before merging with a similar way to rise to a junction with an access road. Go right, above a house to a stile where further flags lead to another enclosed path at a seat. From this path junction take a walled snicket rising left, easing out between houses onto Popples Common.

Turn right on a path along the edge to join a road just short of a junction at Slack with a splendid milestone and a former chapel. Go right just a few strides, then after a few cottages an enclosed path drops left between fields, with Hebden Dale ahead. The path drops to the edge of Hebden Wood, but without entering take a stile on the left. Across a field bottom the path enters the wood, soon beginning a short descent. Its level course resumes a short way down, and is maintained until a further descent to run on to the hairpin bend of a wide track. Turn up this old route for a steady climb, leaving the trees at a gate to rise back to the start.

Looking south over Colden from Heptonstall Moor

14 CRIMSWORTH DEAN

3½ miles from Midgehole

An easy walk with super woodland and beck scenery

Start New Bridge (GR: 988291), National Trust's Hardcastle Crags car park
Map OS Explorer OL21, South Pennines

From the car park re-cross the bridge and take a narrow way climbing behind the WCs. At a solitary house ignore both its drive slanting away and a continuing climbing track, instead take a gate on the left from where a grass track rises steadily away. After a spell between walls it narrows to a path, crossing open pasture between converging woodland. At the far end it squeezes beneath a dam wall into trees. Go left with an old drain, opening out to trace another drained dam to where a fuller one begins. Here take a path crossing the concrete dividing wall to rise left through trees to join a level path. Go left, dropping slightly but generally undulating through the wood, encouraged by yellow blobs on trees. The path rises steadily to run to a junction just short of a wall at the end. A stile out of the trees sends the path across colourful pasture, through a small gate where flags help with a moist section, then across to a stile into the grounds of a house at Wheat Ing. The flagged path runs to a small gate into the garden proper. Passing right of the house, take its dead-straight drive steeply up the valley side with big views.

At a hairpin bend go straight on a thin path into trees, slanting quickly up to a wall-stile into a field. Slant right, the path fading but pointing to the opposite wall. Ascend to its top corner, taking a stile to trace the fieldtops away left, past Upper Smallshaw Farm and on towards a house, Barker Cote. Having swapped wall-sides en route, don't enter its yard but keep on to the field corner. A stile puts you onto its drive, but as it turns up onto a road, the path strictly endures a complicated two minutes by taking a stile ahead into the buildings at Gib. Passing the first of these advance to the main house, turn up the near side to a small gate into a field, then left a short way to a gap-stile into undergrowth above the house. Another stile puts you onto a short drive out past farm buildings onto Haworth Old Road. Go briefly left to find an enclosed path descending steeply to Crimsworth Dean Beck, turning right at the bottom to Lumb Bridge and Lumb Hole waterfall. The stone-arched packhorse bridge and waterfalls form a delectable scene. Across the bridge a path rises away downstream, but as the main path climbs steeply right between walls, pass through an old gateway in front onto a narrower path. Stoodley Pike is seen far ahead.

     Remaining parallel with the beck the path contours through bracken-filled pastures, meeting a sturdy wall-stile at the end. Passing the rear of humble Outwood follow its grassy drive to a gate into NT woodland. Ignore this however in favour of a gap to its left, and a part-flagged path slants down the field to a stile into woods. A path runs down to stone-arched Weet Ing Bridge: don't cross, but continue on the same bank, rising a little then running towards a gate into a field. One hundred paces before it however, rise right on a thinner but clear path slanting to join a drive. Follow this left all the way back down to Midgehole. Early open views are enjoyed, and beyond an old quarry a firmer access road comes in. Into trees this becomes surfaced for the final stage.

In Crimsworth Dean

15 HARDCASTLE CRAGS

4 miles from Midgehole

Renowned woodlands on the edge of Hebden Bridge

Start *New Bridge (GR: 988291), National Trust's Hardcastle Crags car park*
Map *OS Explorer OL21, South Pennines*

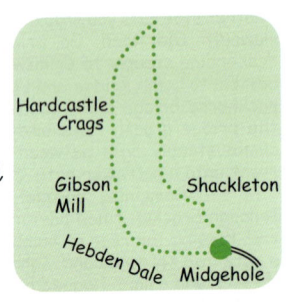

Hardcastle Crags is the name by which everyone knows the valley of Hebden Dale, through which flows Hebden Water. The majority of this richly wooded, deep-cut dale is in the care of the National Trust, and draws crowds from far and wide. The 'Crags' themselves are actually visited on this walk. From the bottom car park head up the drive a few strides until just past a solitary lodge, then fork left on a path descending to Hebden Water. Here a wide path is met and accompanied upstream for almost a mile and a half to Gibson Mill, only straying from the bank to circumvent a couple of short, impassable sections. After a splendid lengthy beckside spell you rise again (both options soon merge) to run to a T-junction. Drop back to the beck at stepping-stones (not used), from where the last stage is an unbroken stroll upstream to the mill. Two further sets of stepping-stones are passed, giving options to trace the opposite bank for a short spell. A 'psalm-plaque' adorns a rock in the beck just before the final stones as the mill appears ahead.

Gibson Mill was founded in 1800 as a water-powered cotton mill. Later enlarged, it ceased to operate in the 1890s, becoming a curiously-sited dance hall and even a roller-skating rink during the mid-20th century. The well-preserved building is an imposing sight in its wooded environs, and features a small cafe, WC, shop and information, as well as exhibitions. Related features include a row of workers' cottages, while a stone-arched bridge spans the beck. Around the back is a millpond and cut. Rejoining the drive to climb above the beck, it levels out alongside the steep rise of Hardcastle

Crags. These invite an ungainly scramble just up to the left. The modest outcrops occupy a prominent knoll bedecked with clumps of heather, with a tiny ridge rising above the treetops. As a result this airy spot is a superb vantage point.

Continuing on from the crags, remain on the track as it swings uphill to merge with a firmer access road at the wood top. Turn right on this for a mile and a half's easy stroll to the hamlet of Shackleton. Immediately before the first building take a gate on the right, with the wooded gulf of Hebden Dale below. Dropping away, a narrow, grassy way quickly forms between old walls, down to a stile at the bottom back into the top of the woods. Firstly go a few strides right onto the crest of a gritstone crag, a splendid viewpoint. Back at the stile, take the path dropping left beneath the wall, within a minute reaching a path junction. Keep left, slanting grandly down a substantially causeyed old way. This drops at a good gradient through the wood, reaching the corner of a large open pasture. Keeping above it you quickly leave the trees to become pleasantly enclosed, still largely on the old causey. At the bottom it empties you back into the wood, with the car park just below.

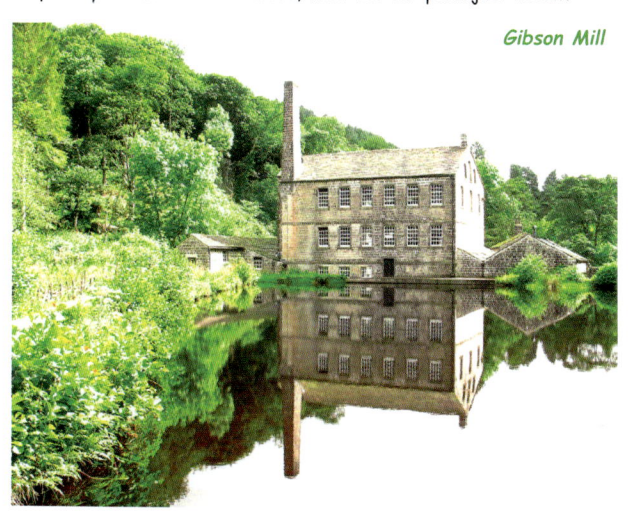

Gibson Mill

16 HEPTONSTALL

*2¾ miles
from Hebden Bridge*

**A steep haul to a classic
old village: dramatic views**

Start Town centre
(GR: 991272), car parks
Map OS Explorer OL21, South Pennines

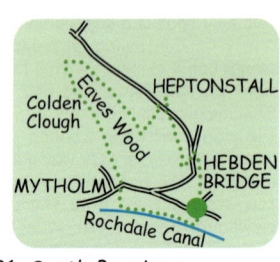

Across the stone-arched bridge in the centre linking the White Swan with the Hole in't Wall, cross to climb a steep cobbled way, The Buttress. With big views back over town it ascends relentlessly onto a level road. Go left a few strides to an old milestone at a junction, then ascend a rough access road opposite. Beyond the second house it ends at a small quarry site. Just before it, a superb part enclosed path heads off right, rising gently through part wooded surrounds, curving around and up to emerge via the front of a short terrace onto a road at the foot of Heptonstall. Turn left up past the Post office/shop and tearoom.

Heptonstall is a fascinating village steeped in history, and of greater importance than Hebden Bridge until the Industrial Revolution. On the main street (Towngate) turn right on Northgate by the Cross Inn, passing an intriguing wall tablet and along to see the octagonal Wesleyan chapel of 1764, tucked down to the right. Now turn up a back way on the left onto Townfield Lane. Go left past WCs back onto Towngate opposite Weavers Square. Go briefly left, and just past the White Lion go right under an arch on a flagged path to the old church alongside the grammar school of 1772, now a museum. Drop down steps onto a back lane and turn right, emerging at the corner of St Thomas' imposing church.

Go straight ahead towards newer housing, over an access road and on over another. Just past this fork right from the track on a broad path, between new housing to emerge onto the crest of Eaves Wood, revealing dramatic views from gritstone outcrops into

Colden Clough. Stoodley Pike is seen from valley floor to towering monument. Turn right on a splendid high-level path above the wooded clough: take care of youngsters! Keeping to the upper path, the later stages feature a gentle clamber through the bouldery wood top before joining an access road. Turn down this a short way, ignoring a level path striking off right. Just below, as a path crosses the road, double back left into trees. It drops steeply past Lumb Bank Cottage, then down more pleasantly along the base of the wood.

Further, it soon levels out and broadens to run a super course along the foot of Eaves Wood, amid fine beeches. Later, you pass above an incongruous line of red-brick houses, keeping faith with the wood bottom, and on again, arriving above old mill dams. At the end the main way drops down through a gate, and runs a briefly enclosed course down onto an access road at Mytholm. Go left on this, quickly diverted around the right side of the end house, above a steep wooded bank opposite the church. At the end continue through trees (with caution above a steep section) to soon drop down. Merging by old gateposts, it slants down and out onto the main road. Cross and go briefly right: after bridging Colden Water turn down steps as an urban path shadows the beck to its confluence with the Calder. A footbridge across this leads straight ahead and onto the Rochdale Canal towpath. Turn left for a quick return, passing several locks and a massive circular chimney of 1863. Leave just after the canal bridges the river, dropping left onto Holme Street.

Colden Clough from Eaves Wood

17   BROADHEAD CLOUGH

4¼ miles from Mytholmroyd

**Outstanding walking features
Cragg Vale's wooded delights**

Start Village centre (GR: 012259), car park by church
Map OS Explorer OL21, South Pennines

From the main junction cross the bridge on the B6138, past St Michael's church and under the railway. At the Shoulder of Mutton bear left on Scout Road, noting a fine old house on the left. At once turn sharp right up Hall Bank Lane at a Methodist Church. When it turns left just above, at some cottages, instead turn right up a suburban road, on past terraces to its far end. An enclosed path takes over above a steep wooded bank, curving left to more open woodland. Ignore a branch dropping right and stay near the wood top. The path runs on to leave the wood at a stile at the end of the business park above. Without joining the access road turn right on an enclosed path, running a pleasant course outside the wood. Emerging into a field at the end, continue as before to a corner stile, from where steps drop steeply to the B6138.

Cross to the footway and go briefly right to cross Dauber Bridge, then double back left on an unsurfaced access road close by Cragg Brook. It swings right to rise alongside a wooded clough before forking: bear left, a good track running on to appraise the skyline of Broadhead Clough. Entering Spring Wood the drive forks: take neither, but go straight ahead on an inviting path into Broadhead Clough Nature Reserve. Initially flagged, the path winds on and gradually up into the welcoming confines of this fine woodland. A flight of steps precedes easier progress as a fence later comes in on the right. As the trees thin out to be replaced by bracken, the path crosses a stile in the fence, above which a surprise awaits as it climbs to a stake on the rim of the amphitheatre, and the climbing ends on high, open moorland.

Resume by crossing the few strides to an old wall corner behind, and trace a path down the wall's long, scant length across Erringden Moor. Evading moist moments a wall corner is reached at the end. The path slants left down to another corner, then a faint trod bears left across the moor corner, crossing quickly to a fence-stile. Through the crumbling wall behind you start the long descent, initially with a long-abandoned hollow way. The valley floor appears below, with hillside settlements Midgley and Heptonstall prominent.

The old way leads down to a cart track. Go right a few strides to a stile to resume the descent on a path slanting back left. This splendid route drops through colourful open country to a pylon, just beneath which it swings left towards the edge of trees. Along their fringe it turns downhill again, then slants right to a stile onto a drive. From a stile opposite, a thin path drops by a wooded stream. Emerging just past another stile, continue down the field-side to a slab bridge at a tiny confluence. Bear slightly left across the field to a gate in front of trees, joining a walled track leading down to the right. Bear left at the bottom, becoming surfaced to cross railway and river to emerge onto the main road at an old mill. Cross the road to the Rochdale Canal towpath, and turn right for a short walk back into Mytholmroyd. Passing a lock and a couple of stone-arched bridges, leave at steps up to a modern road bridge. Turn right down Midgley Road, with the starting point just to the right.

Broadhead Clough

18 — WITHENS CLOUGH

*4¼ miles
from Cragg Vale*

**Splendid beck scenery,
breezy moorland, big views**

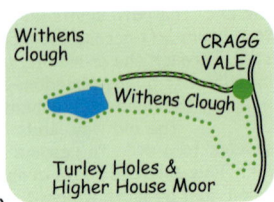

Start Hamlet centre (GR: 999231),
between church and pub beneath main road, roadside parking
Map OS Explorer OL21, South Pennines
Access Open Access land, see page 5

      Cragg Vale's claim to infamy is as the home of the Yorkshire Coiners. It is the most romantically recalled (though far from only) site of 18th century counterfeiting: the practice involved clipping gold from guineas to make additional, inferior coins. Cragg Vale's bleak moorland beginnings soon transform into a deep, richly-wooded valley before joining the Calder Valley at Mytholmroyd. The sombre church of St John the Baptist in the Wilderness dates from 1840, while the adjacent Hinchliffe bar sits in its shadow.
      From the pub advance very briefly along the cul-de-sac clough road, quickly turning left at a surfaced drive climbing away. From a stile at the end of the grounds on the left a broad path crosses to a gate, from where a thinner path runs away, bearing left to the edge of a small wood. It runs on the wood edge to emerge overlooking Cragg Brook. Advance on, ignoring a lower fork to the brook and rising along the wood edge to quickly enter deeper woodland. A superb stride rises steadily and runs high above the stream. Just after a branch drops left, your way is ushered down by a wall to a stile alongside the brook. Enclosed by a wall a path then runs upstream the short way to a clapper-style bridge on the brook. Ignoring the fork that crosses it, instead pass through a small gate in the adjacent wall. Here begins a steep wallside ascent of colourful country aided by a fair portion of stone steps. Easing out at the top with a ruin to the left, pass through an old gateway and a broader way slants gently right up towards Higher House.

Don't enter, but level with it bear left on a path heading away, quickly rising slightly to a stile onto the foot of the grassy Turley Holes and Higher House Moor. Turn right on what proves a splendid path alongside a ditch, rising slightly along the moor edge above woodland. Crossing a brow this then drops very slightly to reveal Withens Clough below, with richly wooded Cragg Vale leading away and Stoodley Pike monument rising over the clough head. Before the slope steepens you meet the end of a catchwater drain: turn left on a superb grassy path tracing its level course all the way along Turley Holes Edge to Withens Clough Reservoir, whose dam soon appears ahead. This was completed in 1894 for Morley Corporation.

For a short-cut simply cross the dam, otherwise resume along the shore, a path quickly bridging a drain to run a grand embanked course alongside the reservoir shore. This leads unfailingly to the head and around to a gate onto the start of a firm track. Turn right on this to quickly return as a walled way outside the reservoir wall, passing the old reservoir keeper's house to reach the northern end of the dam. From here a surfaced road drops back down to the start for a direct, uncomplicated finish.

Cragg Vale from Turley Holes Edge

19 — MIDGLEY MOOR

4$\frac{1}{4}$ miles from Booth

A breezy encounter with splendid heather moorland

Start Jerusalem Farm (GR: 036277), car park half-mile west of Booth village on Jerusalem Lane above Luddenden
Map OS Explorer OL21, South Pennines

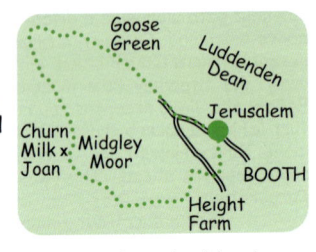

Jerusalem Farm is run by Calderdale Countryside Service, with environmental workshops and campsite. Rejoin the road and drop a few strides to a stile opposite. A good path slants left up a colourful bank to a big wall-stile. Already you enjoy big views over Luddenden Dean. A little path maintains this slant up another steep pasture to the top corner. From the stile go left on the wallside, curving up to a gate into a cobbled yard at some houses. Follow the drive out to a road, noting a neat short-cut on the right just before the end. Go a few strides right to a small gate beneath the row of houses at Green House, and ascend to the garden top where a gate puts you into a field. Ascend directly up the wallside, into a tree-planted enclosure and then up the outside of a garden at Height Farm, with a fence leading to a wall-stile at the top.

This puts you onto the heather of Midgley Moor, and just in front an excellent path runs left above the wall. When a fence takes over remain on the moor, the wall soon returning on a bend. Here you look down on Luddenden Foot in the main valley, and more impressively Cragg Vale, Broadhead Clough and Stoodley Pike. The path leads delightfully on above a lone house until the adjacent wall ultimately drops away: here the path bears gently right to begin a steady rise above old quarries to a wall corner, with the standing stone of Churn Milk Joan just a minute higher at a path junction. This sturdy six-footer has possibly medieval origins, and its hollowed top still sees the leaving of alms.

Leave by the distinct path rising directly away behind the stone, enjoying a gentle rise into the heart of the moor. On easing out, the impressive Bronze Age burial cairn of Millers Grave is seen over to the right. The path runs largely level for a while, and as a boundary stone stands just to the right, views open out left. The path makes a nice, brief descent towards the depression of Dimmin Dale. Ignoring a lesser left branch the way curves down towards the right alongside a sunken way, entering moister terrain at a path crossroads by remains of a shooting butt. Turn right, this broader path passing further old butts and quickly dropping back to the Luddenden side of the moor. Merging with a path from the left, bear right to a crumbling wall corner at the well-defined moor edge giving super views into Luddenden Dean. While a path runs along the edge, yours begins to descend, doubling back briefly to the old wall.

The path enjoys a well-graded slant down to the right, and leaves the moor at a gate just above Goose Green. A splendid green way winds down between walls onto the enclosed track of Wood Lane by a nice house. Turn right on this for a short mile, becoming fully surfaced to rise to a junction with a hairpin bend. Go left to return to Jerusalem Farm.

Churn Milk Joan

20 — LUDDENDEN DEAN

3½ miles from Booth

Absorbing rambling in an unsung valley awash with interest

Start Jerusalem (GR: 036277), car park half-mile west of Booth on Jerusalem Lane above Luddenden
Map OS Explorer OL21, South Pennines

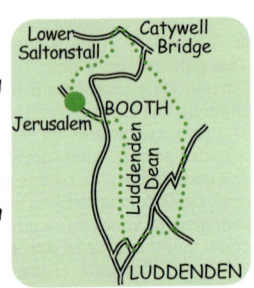

Jerusalem Farm is run by Calderdale Countryside Service, with environmental workshops and campsite. From the farm turn down the road towards Booth. Beyond the trees take a stile on the left to slant down a wallside onto the road through Booth. Cross over and down steps and cobbles to a lower road by houses at Goit Side. Turn right to a cobbled fork at two characterful houses. Bear left, then straight on the broad track. This runs to two final houses, where the bridleway continues into trees to emerge at another row of houses. At the end the access road goes left over the brook, but your way is straight on, narrowing back to a bridleway. This runs a firm course by Luddenden Brook to fork just short of Luddenden village. Either puts you in the centre, the left one via St Mary's church. Luddenden oozes character, at its heart the Lord Nelson pub. Branwell Bronte drank here when employed at Luddenden Foot station.

Turn left down over the bridge, and the road slants up to a junction at a well. Double back left up Stocks Lane, with fine views over the village. At a terrace, pass through a gap at the end, up steps between houses and up into a field. Ascend steeply to a stile at the top right corner, then up a wallside to a corner stile: a path slants left over open ground to a stile onto a road. Just a few strides right is your continuing route on an initially cobbled road, but first go a few strides further to see a splendid old house. The access road, meanwhile, runs on to a short terrace. As it drops away keep straight on a narrow, level bridleway between walls. Passing the front of a house, cross its drive to resume as before,

46

emerging onto a road. Rise right a short way then bear left down an access track. When a branch doubles back left keep straight on to Old Riding Farm.

Entering the yard a path runs on above a barn to a scrubby bank. It slants down to run along the bottom and into woodland. Emerging, it runs round the base of a steep pasture to a stream crossing. Turn sharply uphill outside trees, levelling out at a gate where an enclosed green way runs on, at the other end winding up to houses. Passing one on your right, turn up the access road which jinks then slants left up to a sharp bend: here go straight ahead over a stile. An embanked path runs through small fields to a house, Peace Cote. From a gate onto the drive by the house go straight over to a stile, and a path slants down to a road. Go straight over to a stile, then down a wallside path to a house at Hock Cliff. Pass to its right and head away on a cart track. At the road go left to Catywell Bridge, with the Cat-i-the-Well pub behind.

Only a minute further is the hamlet of Lower Saltonstall: after the first house on the left turn down a drive, passing between houses to a gate into a field. Trace a wall down as far as a gate/stile on the right, then a field-top wall leads to the next stile. Bear left to a gate/stile opposite, from where cross diagonally to a wall-stile. Behind is a little gate into Wade Wood. A thin path slants right, down to a cross-paths: keep straight on down the path ahead to Wade Bridge. Across, go left up the enclosed green way to finish.

Luddenden

HILLSIDE GUIDES... cover much of Northern England

Short Scenic Walks guides (more in preparation)
- UPPER WHARFEDALE · LOWER WHARFEDALE
- UPPER WENSLEYDALE · LOWER WENSLEYDALE
- MALHAMDALE · SWALEDALE · RIBBLESDALE
- INGLETON/WESTERN DALES · SEDBERGH/DENTDALE
- NIDDERDALE · HARROGATE/KNARESBOROUGH
- BOWLAND · AROUND PENDLE · RIBBLE VALLEY
- BORROWDALE · HAWORTH/BRONTE COUNTRY
- ILKLEY/WASHBURN VALLEY · AMBLESIDE/LANGDALE
- AIRE VALLEY · HEBDEN BRIDGE/CALDER VALLEY

Our *Walking Country* range features longer walks...

- WHARFEDALE · MALHAMDALE · WENSLEYDALE
- HARROGATE & the WHARFE VALLEY · SWALEDALE
- RIPON & LOWER WENSLEYDALE · NIDDERDALE
- THREE PEAKS · HOWGILL FELLS · HOWARDIAN HILLS
- TEESDALE · EDEN VALLEY · ALSTON & ALLENDALE

- ILKLEY MOOR · BRONTE COUNTRY · CALDERDALE
- PENDLE & the RIBBLE · WEST PENNINE MOORS
- ARNSIDE & SILVERDALE · LUNESDALE · BOWLAND

- LAKELAND FELLS, SOUTH · LAKELAND FELLS, EAST
- LAKELAND FELLS, NORTH · LAKELAND FELLS, WEST

Long Distance Walks
- COAST TO COAST WALK · CUMBRIA WAY · DALES WAY
- NIDDERDALE WAY · FURNESS WAY · CALDERDALE WAY
- WESTMORLAND WAY · PENDLE WAY · BRONTE WAY

Visit www.hillsidepublications.co.uk
or write for a catalogue